Doing Unto Others

Written and Illustrated by
Ron and Rebekah Coriell

Fleming H. Revell Company
Old Tappan, New Jersey

© 1980 Fleming H. Revell Company
All rights reserved.
Printed in the United States of America

Forgive
give

Treating Someone as Though He Never Hurt Me

Forbearing one another, and forgiving one another, if any man have a quarrel against any: even as Christ forgave you, so also do ye.

Colossians 3:13

Forgiveness in the Bible

The sight was almost too horrible to view. But angry people were looking on as three men were being painfully crucified on the wooden crosses.

The crowd was interested in the man on the center cross. He was Jesus, who called Himself the Son of God. Most of the people did not believe Him. He had done many kind and helpful things for them. But the religious leaders had lied about Jesus and said that He was a troublemaker. They were jealous of Him, because some people followed His teachings and not theirs.

"If He be the King of Israel, let Him now come down from the cross, and we will follow Him," mocked the rulers (Matthew 27:42).

Others said with a sneer, "He trusted in God; let Him deliver Him now, if He will have Him: for He said, I am the Son of God" (Matthew 27:43).

Even one of the two thieves who were crucified on each side of Jesus said unkind words about Him. No one seemed to care about Jesus.

Was Jesus angry with these cruel people? No, He forgave them, because He loved them. As He hung in pain He prayed, "Father, forgive them; for they know not what they do" (Luke 23:34).

This story is found in Matthew 27:35-51; Luke 23:33- 38.

Forgiveness at Home

"I just couldn't wait to tell Father about the birthday present you bought him," explained Robby to his older brother, Dennis.

"But you promised not to tell," replied Dennis. "For weeks I've planned to surprise Father with a new tie."

Robby did not understand how deeply he had hurt his brother's feelings. Dennis slowly walked away. Noticing the sad expression on his face, Mother followed Dennis into his room.

"Do you love your brother?" asked Mother.

Dennis was surprised at her question. "Of course I do," he replied.

"I know you feel that he has not treated you kindly," comforted Mother. "I also know that Jesus was treated unkindly by the people who crucified Him. Yet He showed His love for them by asking His Father to forgive them. A good way in which you could show your love for your brother would be to forgive him. Treat him as if he never hurt you. I know you do not feel like it. But do it anyway, because it is the right thing to do."

Dennis stayed in his room for a while. Then he came out smiling. Dennis did love his brother, and he showed it by forgiving him.

Forgiveness at School

The class was only making one clay project this year. Dennis was proud of his clay turtle, because it looked so real. Someone told him it was the most carefully made project in the class.

Clay has to dry completely before it can be baked hard. Each of the students carefully placed his project on a shelf, so it could dry for a few days. Every day Dennis inspected his turtle to see if it was dry. On Wednesday he discovered that it was broken.

"Who broke my turtle?" Dennis shouted.

Carma stammered, "I — I did, and I — I'm so sorry. I picked it up to look at it, and it slipped out of my hand."

Dennis gave her an angry look and sat down in his chair, in a huff. His teacher talked to him about his attitude: "Dennis, being angry will not put your turtle back together. Being angry at Carma is a way of hurting her. She is sorry that she broke your project. She really needs you to forgive her, so that she will feel better. When you do, you will feel better, too."

Later that day, Dennis took his teacher's advice. He forgave Carma, and they were friends again. Both felt better when Dennis forgave Carma.

Forgiveness at Play

It was hard to stand on the sidelines and watch. Dennis had hoped to play in the game. His coach had promised that he could be a starter; but at the last moment the new boy had arrived, and the coach had allowed him to take Dennis's place.

It sure is unfair for the coach not to let me play, thought Dennis. *I think I had better pray about this, before I get angry.*

Silently, Dennis prayed and asked God to help him. He forgave his coach. He told the Lord that he was even willing to sit out the whole game if that was what was best for the team.

The game ended, and Dennis did not get to play. He felt sad, but he was happy that his team had won. He congratulated everyone, even the coach.

After everyone had left, the coach called to Dennis, "Dennis, I want to tell you something. I know I did not keep my word and let you play. I was wrong. You did not even get angry. That is the kind of player we need. Tomorrow, you will play the whole game."

As Dennis went home he was glad that he had learned how to be forgiving.

Fair
care

Treating Others Equally

. . . observe these things without preferring one before another, doing nothing by partiality.

1 Timothy 5:21

Fairness in the Bible

The ten men were careful not to let anyone come near them. As people approached, they would call out, "Unclean, unclean!" These men were lepers.

One day, Jesus entered the village where the men were. Although they stood far away, the lepers recognized Him. They cried out, "Jesus, Master, have mercy on us!" (Luke 17:13).

Jesus paused to look at the men. Their clothes looked ragged. Their bodies were thin, and they were covered with sores. Nine of the men were Jews, and one was a Samaritan. Most Jews hated Samaritans. They tried not to talk to them. They would not even walk through the land of Samaria. Would Jesus heal only the nine Jews? Or would he treat all ten lepers equally?

Jesus replied, "Go show yourselves unto the priests."

As the ten turned to go, they discovered that they were healed. The Samaritan shouted glory to God. Then he came back to Jesus and fell at His feet. Over and over again, he thanked Him.

Jesus was fair to the ten lepers. He healed them all, even though one was a Samaritan.

This story is found in Luke 17:11-19.

Fairness at Home

Amy squealed with excitement when she heard that her friend, Donna, was coming to spend the night. But Amy's younger sister, Tammy, just frowned.

"It will be wonderful," said Amy. "We will practice our spelling words together, ride bicycles, listen to records, and play some games."

Tammy said nothing. She just looked at the floor. Amy talked about all that she and her friend would do together.

Noticing that her sister did not seem to be happy for her, Amy asked, "What is the matter? Aren't you happy for me, Tammy?"

Tammy paused. The words didn't want to come out. At last she grumbled, "You are not being fair. All afternoon and evening you are going to play with Donna. She is my friend, too. You talk as if you do not want me to play with you and Donna."

Amy felt guilty about her words. She was talking as if Donna were her only playmate. She did want her sister to join them in the fun-filled day.

"I'm sorry, Tammy," said Amy. "Forgive me for not treating you fairly. You will always be my best friend. I want us both to have a good time with our guest tomorrow."

Fairness at School

Amy sat alone on the school steps. All her friends were busy talking to Cindy, the new girl who had come to school that day. She was dressed so nicely. Some of the boys forgot to play kickball; they were too busy trying to get the new girl's attention.

"Recess is no fun today," muttered Amy. "I wish Cindy had not come. I'm not going to fuss over her, like those kids are doing!"

Mr. Whiston, the playground supervisor, walked up to Amy. "You look lonely," he said.

"I am," responded Amy.

"Don't you want to join the others?" he questioned.

"No," she answered. "I'm not going to treat that new girl specially. I don't even like her."

"Then you are not being fair to her," he said. "If you ignore her, you are treating her *very* specially. And you will not get to know her and find out if she would be a nice friend. Why not be fair and give her a chance?"

Mr. Whiston's words made sense. The other children did look as if they were having fun with Cindy.

All right, I'll be fair and treat Cindy just like all my friends, thought Amy as she ran over to join the group.

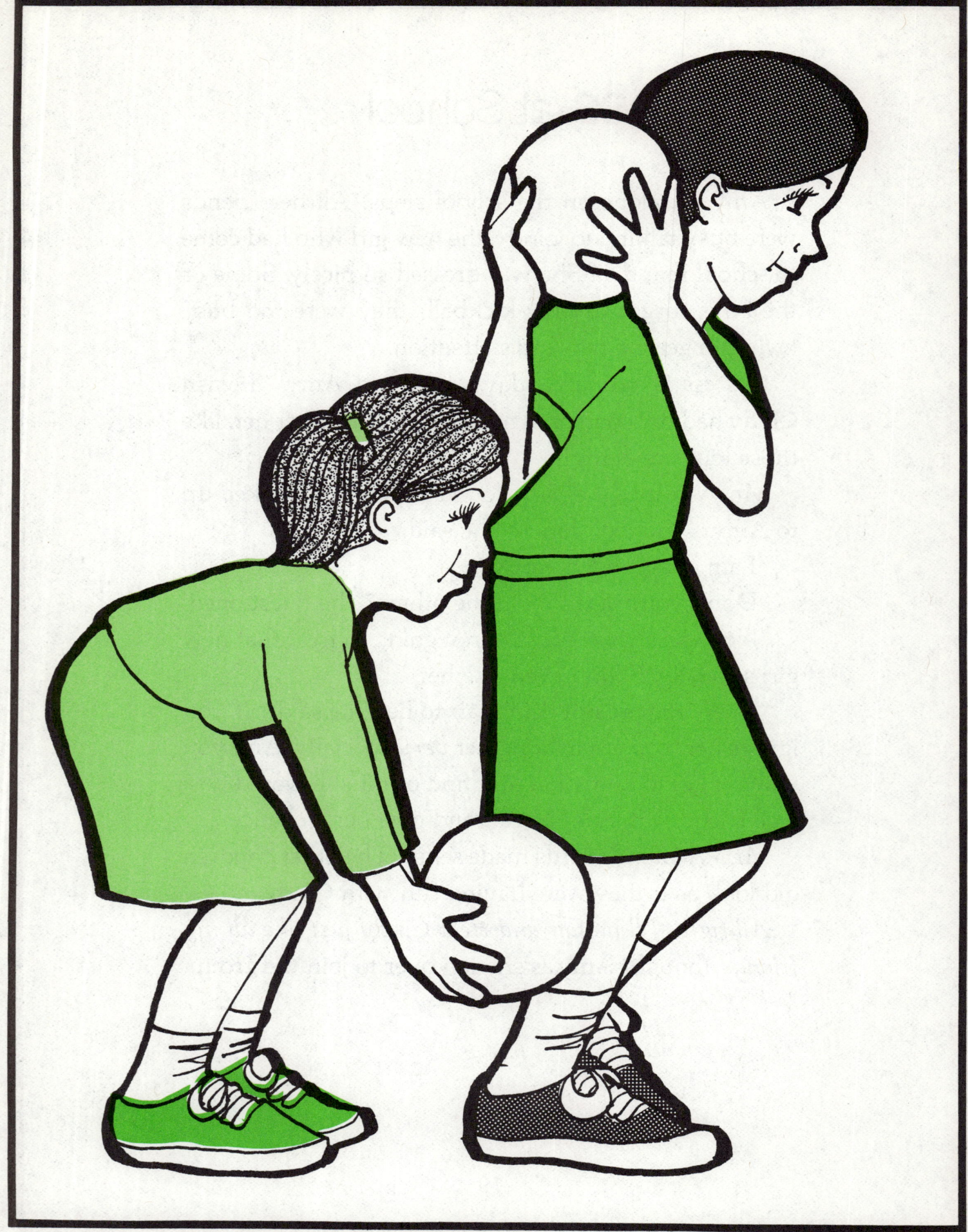

Fairness at Play

Dodge ball is one of Amy's favorite games. She plays it every Saturday with her friends at the park. One day she was especially having fun, because she was winning almost all the games. She could throw and catch the ball very well.

As they played, Amy noticed that a little friend named Trudy always seemed to be the first girl out. She was not a fast runner, and she could not throw or catch the ball well. The older girls always threw the ball at her first.

"That is so unfair," said Amy to a friend on her team. "She must not have very much fun being hit first."

"But how can we help that?" asked her friend.

"I have an idea," said Amy.

She whispered in her teammate's ear. Then they picked up the balls and began the game. They stayed near Trudy. The older girls on the other team didn't dare hit Trudy now. They were afraid Amy would get them out. Trudy had so much fun in that game. She even got some other girls out. Amy's heart was glad because now Trudy was being treated more fairly.

Tolerant
elephant

Accepting Others, Even if They Are Different

My brethren, have not the faith of our Lord Jesus Christ, the Lord of glory, with respect of persons.

James 2:1

Tolerance in the Bible

Jesus was often invited into people's homes for dinner. He would meet many different families and would teach them about God. On one occasion He was asked into the home of two sisters who were as different as night and day.

Martha had a servant's spirit and was always looking for a way to help others. With great joy she began to collect the things she would need to cook a delicious meal for Jesus.

On the other hand, her sister, Mary, was a learner. She knew that Jesus was a great teacher. She was excited about hearing Him speak to her in person. Cooking and serving dinner were the furthest things from her mind. Eagerly she sat near Jesus and began to listen as He talked.

Martha became troubled. She said, "Lord, dost Thou not care that my sister hath left me to serve alone? Bid her, therefore, that she help me" (Luke 10:40).

Jesus told her in a kind way not to be worried about Mary. She had wisely chosen to listen to His teaching.

Jesus knew that Martha wanted to be a helper. Therefore, He was tolerant of her complaint and did not get angry. He accepted her even though she was different from her sister, Mary.

This story is found in Luke 10:38-42.

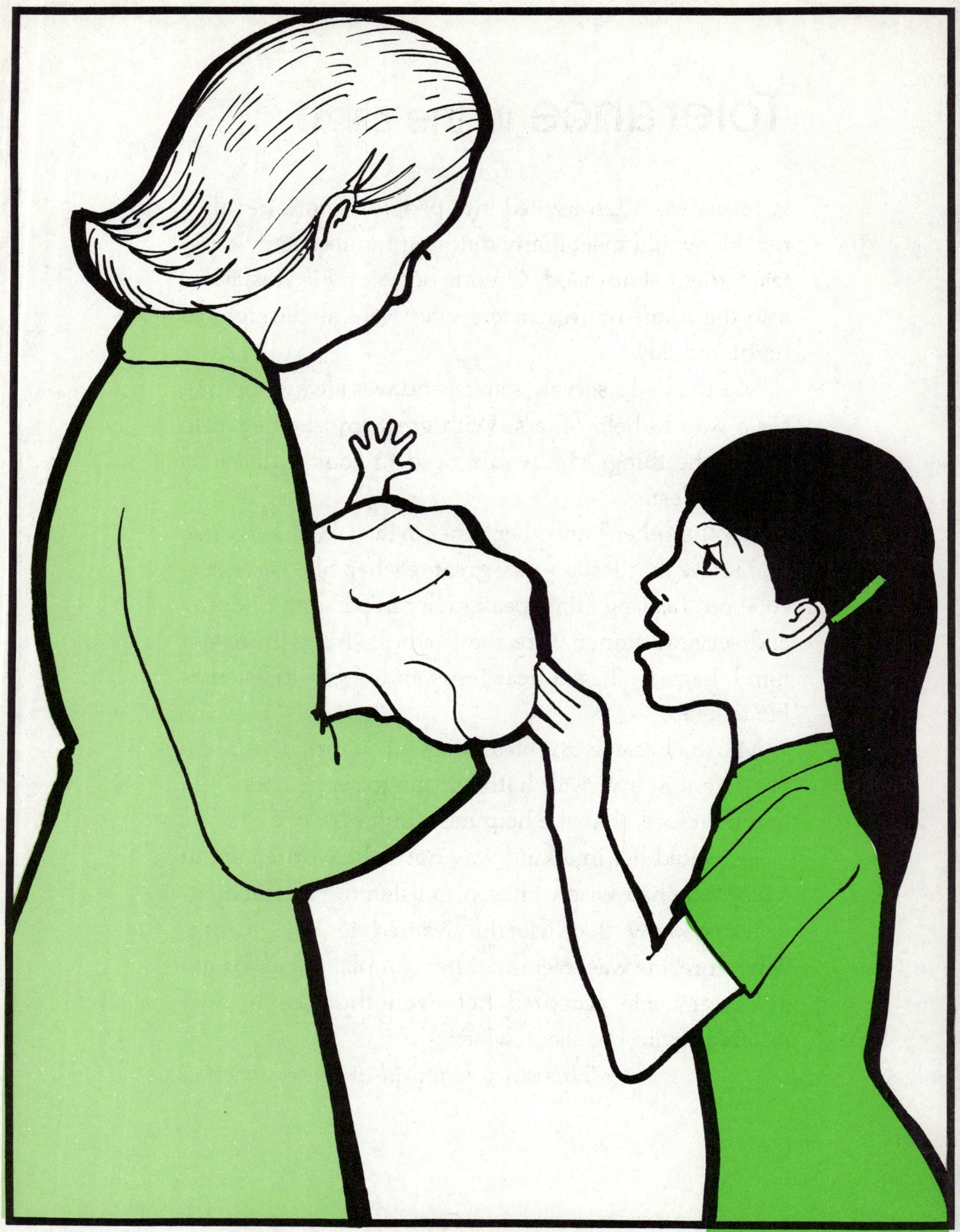

Tolerance at Home

Pamela waited eagerly for mother to arrive home with Teresa, the new baby. She had prayed a long time for a new sister. Now, at last, she would have one.

However, all her dreams and hopes were shattered when her mother brought the baby home. She was a different kind of baby. Pamela's mother told her that her new sister had been born with a withered arm and that it would never grow to be normal. She would never be able to play baseball or sew.

Pamela was really ashamed of Teresa. She did not like to look at her or even want to show her to her friends.

Noticing Pamela's wrong attitude, her mother encouraged her, "Pamela, God made Teresa just the way she is. God never makes a mistake. He must have a special purpose for her life. We don't undertand it now, but maybe we will later. I hope you will be more tolerant of her and learn to love her as well."

As Pamela watched her parents lovingly take care of her new sister and daily thank God for her, Pam's attitude toward her began to change. Soon she was asking to help hold, feed, and rock her.

Pamela was learning to accept Teresa, even though she was different; and, as a result, God helped her to develop a special love for her new baby sister.

Tolerance at School

"Students, I would like you to meet a new classmate," announced Mrs. Baker, the teacher. "Her name is Susie Wong and she is from China. I'm sure you will want to get to know her."

As Susie took her seat some of Pamela's friends giggled. The new girl did not hear them.

During recess, Pamela asked her friends what was so funny.

"She's not like us," said one friend. "She looks different and she talks funny."

"That is no reason to laugh at her," responded Pamela.

"Well, if you want to be her friend, go ahead," they said. "We don't want to be friends with a girl who looks and talks differently."

Pamela was sorry that her friends were not more tolerant. She did not let this stop her from becoming friends with the new girl.

Pamela soon found that Susie was very friendly and very talented. She taught Pamela how to paint pretty flowers with watercolors. She also taught her some Chinese words.

Being tolerant helped Pamela to understand and enjoy a new friend.

Tolerance at Play

Pamela was disappointed. Her mother told her that they would have to baby-sit a neighbor two afternoons a week, while her parents were at work. The neighbor, Carol Connors, was handicapped with polio. She had to use crutches in order to walk.

"Mother, how can we have fun together if she cannot ride a bike, swim, or run?" asked Pamela.

"You will just have to find other things to do," replied Mother.

Pamela accepted her mother's words and decided to try to be tolerant of her new playmate.

On Tuesday, Pamela spent her first afternoon with Carol. Time passed very slowly. The girls didn't know what to do together.

Finally, Carol said, "Let me show you how to play my harmonica. I'm taking lessons now."

Pamela's parents could not afford music lessons. However, Carol was willing to teach Pamela everything that she was learning. An inexpensive harmonica was bought for Pamela. Before long, she and Carol could play duets.

"Carol is so much fun," Pamela told her mother one day, after Carol had gone home. "At first it wasn't easy for me to accept playing with a crippled friend."

"Yes," replied Mother. "But God will always help us to be tolerant, if we are willing to try."

Character Development Challenges

This page is designed to give parents and teachers practical suggestions for teaching character traits to children.

Forgiveness

1. Encourage the child to do good to someone whom he needs to forgive (Matthew 5:44).
2. Each time a child comes to report a wrongdoing, ask him if he has forgiven the person who has hurt him. If he has not, help him to pray to God, forgiving the person who has harmed him.
3. When a child is unwilling to forgive, ask him to recall a situation in which he needed forgiveness from God and encourage the child to forgive as he has been forgiven.

Fairness

1. Whenever an item is divided among children, allow one child to cut or divide it. Give the first choice to the other children.
2. The child should memorize Proverbs 15:3, to remind him that God is watching to see if he is fair.
3. Explain Christ's words, "So the last shall be first, and the first last . . ." (Matthew 20:16). Use this verse as a motivation for the child to put others before himself.

Tolerance

1. The child should recognize three good characteristics in the life of a person whom he needs to tolerate.
2. Invite into the home or classroom someone from a different country, who can share different customs and life-styles.
3. Acquaint the child with the life story of the blind hymn writer Fanny Crosby. Help him see that someone with a physical handicap has the same emotions and desires that the child experiences.